# THE ART OF
# THE CONDUCTOR

The Definitive Guide to
Music Conducting Skills,
Terms, and Techniques

## JOHN WATKINS

iUniverse, Inc.
New York  Lincoln  Shanghai

# The Art of the Conductor
### The Definitive Guide to Music Conducting Skills, Terms, and Techniques

iUniverse books may be ordered through booksellers or by contacting:

iUniverse
2021 Pine Lake Road, Suite 100
Lincoln, NE 68512
www.iuniverse.com
1-800-Authors (1-800-288-4677)

Because of the dynamic nature of the Internet, any Web addresses or links contained in this book may have changed since publication and may no longer be valid.

The views expressed in this work are solely those of the author and do not necessarily reflect the views of the publisher, and the publisher hereby disclaims any responsibility for them.

ISBN: 978-0-595-43396-4 (pbk)
ISBN: 978-0-595-87721-8 (ebk)

Printed in the United States of America

# THE ART OF
# THE CONDUCTOR

# CONTENTS

# OVERTURE

With the advent of the twentieth century and the explosion of the recording and entertainment industries, there came a vast change in the leisure activities of the general public in the Western world. "Whisker radios" led the charge, followed by moving pictures, and then "talkies." It wasn't long before "radio-grams" were on the market, which gave their owners many choices. By listening to records, people could hear distinguished orchestras, opera companies, folk and lieder singers, or jazz and dance bands. Or, by tuning in to radio broadcasts, they could be entertained by instrumental or vocal performers of the highest calibre. Radios later evolved into high-fidelity stereos (hi-fis), and moving-picture technology grew to incorporate wide-screen, colour, and surround-sound formats. The "home-theatre" experience followed with the appearance of the television.

Before the twentieth century, there was always a hard core of the general public who would attend local performances of oratorio, operetta, orchestral, or band concerts. However, fine concert halls were definitely out of reach for the large rural population, and any advanced knowledge of music was limited to a few.

Lovers of music had previously gathered together and made their own music. They would meet in each other's homes to have "sing-songs" around the family piano. Some would join a local church choir, choral group, or instrumental ensemble. But now, with the advent of recording and broadcasting technologies, they could augment their musical experiences by seeing and hearing the finest professional performers right in their own living rooms.

A concert performance was only too recently the exclusive realm of the privileged class, and attending an opera or symphony concert was a white-tie-and-formal-gown affair. With the coming of the twentieth-century, the opportunity presented itself to ordinary citizens and rural dwellers—even those with no previous interest in or aptitude for music—to have first-hand experience of an art form that had been quite inaccessible, and possibly, due to the absence of exposure, foreign to their tastes.

"Promenade concerts" were first introduced to London, England, in 1895. They were conceived by Robert Newman, whose aim had been to educate the public in easy stages. The idea was to begin with popular music and gradually introduce the classical and modern repertoires.

Sir Henry Wood conducted the first promenade concert in an informal atmosphere at the "Royal Albert Hall." He was encouraged by the response to the availability of cheap tickets for the arena—the central part of the concert hall—where people could stand or sit on the floor immediately in front of the orchestra. Cheap tickets were also available for the upper gallery—which, by the way, is no place for anyone with a fear of heights.

Later in the series, audiences were treated to performances led by many other conductors, such as Malcolm Sargent, John Barbirolli, Charles Groves, and Colin Davis, to name a few. A tradition was established of having a "Wagner Night" on Wednesdays, a "Beethoven Night" on Fridays, and always a special, fun-filled programme for the "Last Night of The Proms."

The class barriers were down, and now Beethoven wasn't just the composer of the "Moonlight Sonata"—the slow movement of which is an all-time favourite of budding young pianists—but had been recognized as a giant among musicians. He was only one of many highly accomplished composers formerly little known to the general population. The masses were suddenly exposed to musical masterpieces far in advance of the traditional ballads and country dances that, along with church music, had previously been their main musical diet.

In the early twentieth century, Hollywood also presented operetta and musical extravaganzas to the public. One of these was "One Hundred Men and a Girl," in which Deanna Durbin sang with the backing of a hundred-piece orchestra conducted by Leopold Stokowski, one of the finest conductors of the day.

No longer was the conductor just a machinelike beater of time. A metamorphosis was taking place—the conductor's role was changing. Towards the end of the nineteenth century, conductors—many of whom were also brilliant instrumentalists and composers—were becoming part of the administration staff of fine orchestras, and their positions were becoming full-time engagements.

This new breed of conductor started to teach special orchestral skills to the instrumentalists. They led their orchestras with an intense creative and emotional drive, and they established an entirely new way of making music. Between 1880 and 1885, Hans von Bülow (1830–1894) built the Meiningen orchestra into one of the best in Germany. Gustav Mahler (1860–1911) was also considered one of the finest of modern conductors.

Later, in the 1920s and '30s, other great conductors like Beecham, Reiner, Toscanini, Monteux, and Koussevitzky—some of whom were quite controversial characters—were noted for setting very high orchestral standards. Fortunately, their recordings could also be heard on gramophone and radio.

The opportunity to watch and listen to works of the masters being played by world-class orchestras created a new generation of music-lovers. Listeners were developing the ability to make their own informed judgements about the quality of a performance, as regards both instrumental skill and the interpretation of the piece. This leads us to a discussion of the role and the art of the conductor.

*Notes:*

"Whisker radios"—also known as crystal radios or crystal sets—were first built in the early 1900s. For the signal detector, they used a metallic mineral such as galena and a fine pointed wire known as a "cat's whisker".

"Radiograms" were usually well finished wooden cabinets which contained both a radio and a gramophone.

# INTRODUCTION

## *EVOLUTION OF AN ART FORM*

It is difficult for the uninitiated to appreciate the finer points of an art that, in its technique, appears to be mysteriously silent. Conversely, an instrumentalist's contribution thrills and moves us with its complex mosaic of sound. Yet without the silent gestures of the baton or hand, body language, facial expression, and eye contact, the conductor's ability to interpret and direct would be in serious trouble. However, it was not always so. Lully, the founder of French grand opera, pounded on the floor with a big stick. Others used violin bows or tightly rolled pieces of manuscript paper to beat out a tempo.

It wasn't until the early nineteenth century that composers such as Mendelssohn started to develop the modern method of conducting. They used highly visible batons and a special convention of signals. This modern technique of beating time is concerned with much more than just maintaining a suitable tempo. It involves starting and stopping, speeding up and slowing down, changing volume, signalling special effects such as *ritenuto* and *fermata*, and, of the utmost importance, cueing soloists or various sections of the ensemble.

For a conductor to attain the requisite level of expertise, the technique must be learned and drilled until it becomes automatic. Any technical hesitancy or error on the part of the conductor would be transmitted immediately to the instrumentalists or choristers, causing feelings of uncertainty—or even panic. This would instantly destroy any hope of a dramatic, emotional, or expressive performance. Once the baton technique has been perfected, however, it becomes a subconscious action as unforgettable as riding a bicycle. But only after this has been achieved can the conductor concentrate on the interpretive side of his job and reproduce, through instrument and voice, the effect that the composer had conceived in his mind and painstakingly drafted into a manuscript.

By the time an original music score has had its early readings, corrections, and rewrites, it can be considered to be finished. The conscientious conductor will try to create a faithful reproduction using the composer's instructions for dynamics and expression. It is unfortunate that some "pseudo-virtuoso" conductors consider their version of a piece superior to that of the composer's. These conductors ride the composer's coattails and try to capture personal glory with extravagances of style and mannerism. They are often praised by the undiscerning in the audience and by those who enjoy sensationalism. In fact, these conductors are betraying the composer—they are using the composer's work to satisfy their own egos.

Having said that, it is interesting to note that Handel's great classic, "Messiah," was rewritten many times. The version heard most frequently today was prepared and arranged by Wolfgang Amadeus Mozart.

Composers must be well acquainted with the technical peculiarities of each instrument or voice for which they are writing. What lies comfortably on one could well be almost impossible on another and cause untold grief for the player.

Also, composers have to be very precise in the scoring of their music, so that the performer has no doubt as to the composer's intentions. Maurice Ravel was once upset that a pianist had taken unpardonable liberties with his "Piano Concerto for Left Hand." In this instance however, the pianist hadn't just been interpreting—he had been rewriting.

Unless he is conducting a performance of his own composition, the consummate conductor's task is not to create, but to recreate. To do this, the successful conductor must be:

1.  Highly knowledgeable about the voices and instruments that the composer has used, be they brass, woodwind, string, organ, voice, or any of those many devices which come under the heading of percussion—even cannon fire, if necessary.

2.  Extremely cognizant of the principles and language of the notation used in the scoring process.

Without this knowledge, the conductor would be unable to interpret—that is, to faithfully recreate—the score. He or she would be unable to send the correct signals or to describe the desired effects in terms of the player's own area of expertise.

The performance of an orchestral or choral concert is an extremely complicated affair, especially when one considers the day-to-day physiological variances in all the people involved. Rehearsals are therefore a necessity, as they enable the anticipation and resolution of all potential technical problems.

Conductors need practice, too. By the time of the performance, everyone involved must be sufficiently imbued with a confidence that can only come from having done it well during practice. At first, it is better to practise the correct notes, even at a slower pace, than to practise wrong notes. Only then can the full potential of the music be realized, the parts become a whole, and the whole be fully developed with all the appropriate nuances. However, a good leader can motivate the ensemble members to practise notes in their own time. This will allow rehearsal time to be fully utilised for the improvement of all the *other* aspects of the performance.

And so, through some enigmatic magic and under a spell of inspiration, the conductor summons up prodigious powers of communication. He sends seemingly telepathic messages to those under his direction and brings forth a continuous blending of sounds to match his inner imaginings, and he or she does all this with silent gestures, facial expressions, and body language.

# *VARIOUS FORMS OF MUSIC*

Conducting an orchestra, ballet, choir, band, or any combination of these groups requires the same techniques, with possibly only slight variances between them. Some purely choral conductors do not use a baton. They prefer to convey their messages with the hands, feeling that the stick restricts their ability to convey some signals peculiar to the voice.

However, we must remember that a choral member, who may be singing from memory, has a greater opportunity than an instrumentalist to watch every move of the conductor. The latter must rely to a greater extent on peripheral vision as a means of receiving the conductor's signals. Peripheral vision is more likely to detect the motion of a long white stick than a subtle twist of the wrist or movement of the fingers, especially when the lighting is rather poor, as it may well be in the orchestra pit of a theatre.

The average instrumentalist also has more of a solo role than a chorister and has less opportunity to be a follower in the group dynamics. The instrumentalist must therefore be more independent and spend more time with eyes glued to the music, counting off tacet passages and timing the next entry. Awareness of the conductor's baton is imperative.

The main difference between conducting various ensembles of the same calibre regards not the type of group, but its size and complexity. The variables introduced by dissimilar ensembles, while not requiring different technique, change the number of items which come under the conductor's area of responsibility and control.

A very small group, such as a quintet of instruments or a vocal duet with piano, may find a conductor useful during early practices while learning the music, but is better off without one during a performance.

To achieve a harmonious performance, such artists have to learn different skills, such as listening very closely to one another with acute awareness and receptivity, and adapting to each other's volume, rhythm, and tempo. This is a different art—the art of ensemble playing as required in chamber groups.

A very large orchestra requires more attention by the conductor than would a small theatre orchestra. For a large orchestra, it would not only be necessary to cue the strings, woodwinds, brass, and drum set, but also the timpani, wood-blocks, xylophone, harp, organ, and any other effect required by the score.

However, a small theatre-pit orchestra, when combined with a group of actors and chorus members performing an operetta, could demand a lot more attention than a large orchestra. The conductor would have to follow the libretto (or at least have libretto cues on the score), know when to bring in the orchestra after periods of dialogue, cue the entrances of on-stage principals, chorus, and orchestra members, and coordinate the activities of the musicians with those of the actors.

The medium of dance introduces yet another variable, not only for ballet productions but also for choreographed portions of musical theatre. Although conducting technique may not change for dance, it requires that the conductor have a feeling for the problems that a dancer may encounter when performing difficult movements. While in midair, a dancer cannot adjust to the introduction of an unexpected *tenuto*, or holding of a note. The music must help, not hinder, the artist's performance.

# CONDUCTORS' ATTRIBUTES

Since the success of conductors often depends in large measure on their ability to study and memorize long passages of music, they usually specialize in certain types of work, such as symphonic or operatic. But, in whichever genre they practice, they must all share common attributes. For example, good physical conditioning is essential for standing for long periods while vigorously moving about on the podium with arms raised.

An interesting experiment may be carried out by measuring the amount of time it takes to tire the muscles when holding one's arms out at shoulder height. It is preferable to use a podium with the music just above waist height. This is high enough to enable one to glance down at the music with very little movement of the head and to allow the elbows to be relaxed into the body for an occasional rest. This is harder to do when not using a baton as an extension of the forearm.

Another essential attribute of the conductor is the ability to create the music in the mind in parallel with the orchestra or ensemble. One is unable to beat out a rhythm against opposing forces unless one can internalize the music—by singing inwardly, or imagining a marching stride or the dancer's sequence—and keep time with an internal metronome. Only then can the conductor be as strong as a machine in controlling something with a will of its own.

Musicians—both instrumentalists and singers—have a tendency to rush passages of many small notes and thus get ahead of the beat. This, of course, is less noticeable with professionals, as they spend many hours learning to accurately subdivide beats into equal groupings of three, four, five, and so forth. The subconscious temptation for the conductor—one that must be vigorously resisted—is to go along with the faster beats, which forces a gradual increase in the tempo of the whole ensemble.

The conductor must be an excellent reader of music and knowledgeable about the many Italian or German, terms and expressions used in a score. Giovanni Ricordi was one of the first publishers of mass-produced sheet music, and his Italian instructions and terms soon became the accepted norm. However, lieder by composers such as Schubert often used the German language.

Learning to play one or more instruments gives one a good grounding in reading music, especially when the instrument is the piano. While playing the piano, the mind has to interpret two different staves at once: the treble and the bass. Also, familiarity with instrumentalists' endeavours and problems is essential to be able to conduct their playing.

When he or she is dealing with an amateur organization, the conductor should also be able to suggest to particular instrumentalists ways of achieving certain effects, and explain himself in a manner that can be easily understood by that group. For example, a wind player struggling with breathing and embouchure problems would not need the same advice as a string player with bowing-technique problems. A good conductor must be a good teacher.

Although it is often said that "If you can hear yourself playing, you are playing too loud," this is rather an exaggeration. Without some sort of audible feedback, it is impossible to make personal adjustments. But it is true to say that, "If you can hear yourself playing, you may be playing off key—or *someone* is." Loud playing or singing, often leads to intonation errors. With a keen ear or "perfect pitch," the conductor should immediately recognize and correct any such problems. However, intonation problems are less frequent in the better orchestras, because the audition and selection processes should already have weeded out those with pitch-recognition difficulties.

To a large degree, conducting is an authoritative process wherein the will of one overrules the inclinations of the many.

However, this is more the case during performances than during rehearsals. During rehearsals, the conductor has the opportunity to earn the respect and cooperation of those under his direction. If leadership skills can be successfully demonstrated during rehearsals, and problems are ironed out without the conductor being too autocratic or dictatorial, then his baton will be followed more willingly and faithfully during performances. Indeed, it is better for the conductor to think of him/herself as a facilitator whose object is to help the musicians perform at their best.

As has been mentioned before, a conductor must be able to internalize the desired tempo and hold it as though the mind and muscles were controlled by a metronome. There are many diversions and distractions to deal with—audience reactions, interruptions, and individual instrumental problems, for example. It is of paramount importance for the conductor to be able to stay focussed on the task at hand using strong powers of concentration.

Conducting a large orchestra or ensemble can be compared to propelling a heavy load with a small stick. It feels as though you are dealing with an immovable object. It's only strength of will and delicate balancing that enable the conductor to direct the outcome of his or her wishes. When the conductor attempts to control an *accelerando* or *rallentando*, for example, one section of an orchestra or chorus often follows the stick better than another. Without extreme care, this problem can lead to separation of the sections and final collapse, and so it requires great skill and a cool head to overcome.

Getting someone else to do voluntarily what you want them to do involves teamwork. The best team leaders are empathetic toward their team members. The ability to share another's emotions, thoughts, and feelings is a strong contributor to the conductor's success. The conductor must be sufficiently pliable to lead the show while simultaneously adjusting to the needs of the moment, empathizing with soloists, knowing when to switch from leading to following, and recovering from potential disasters.

It is of growing importance these days that a conductor also act as master of ceremonies for a concert—to gain an early rapport with the audience, to give some notes on the programme, and to introduce guest artists. This requires a pleasant disposition, an engaging and entertaining manner, and good presentation skills.

The conductor is such a prominent figure during a performance that the audience must be able to feel very comfortable with him or her and be able to relax and enjoy the concert. Any negative feeling on the side of the audience will surely be transmitted back to the ensemble. On the other hand, a comfortable audience seems to project a pleasant and powerful aura that can be highly infectious.

And so we see that the consummate conductor must be a magician and a visionary with almost clairvoyant, super-sensory powers. A conductor must have the ability to infect the ensemble with the correct mood and, at the same time, have a complete working knowledge of every detail of the orchestra or choir. But that's not all—without a strong, impeccable conducting technique, all good intentions will be in vain.

# TECHNIQUE

## *THE BATON*

Some conductors prefer not to use a baton, especially choral conductors working at close quarters with the singers. Many choral conductors feel that directing with the hands gives them more flexibility to send messages regarding vocal production and dynamics. They feel restricted when using a baton. These conductors will invariably develop their own particular hand-movements, which, for a resident conductor, might be perfectly adequate. But this might cause problems when a conductor moves from one group to another.

However, it can also be said of many baton-wielding conductors that their techniques are also sufficiently home-grown to be an acquired taste or to require a long learning curve for struggling performers.

The shaft of the baton—which is white and also adds an extra length to the arm—brings with it many advantages over bare hands. Not the least of these is visibility, especially in poorly lit halls where one can barely see a timpanist in the dark, distant corner of the stage or a diminutive horn player struggling to see from behind a row of bassoons. But, more than that, the baton allows great flexibility, requires less effort, and, when held gently in the hand, is easier on the muscles and tendons of the arm and shoulder. It can describe a very visible arc or straight line with no more than a simple rotation or rocking of the wrist.

## Purchasing a Baton

Batons vary in the shape of the handle and in the length of the shaft, so it is advisable to hold a few different ones and test them for feel before making a purchase. Its length can always be shortened with a hacksaw and file if, after being used for a while, it feels too long and clumsy. On the other hand, it is a technical challenge to lengthen a baton that is too short.

The type of baton used is very much a matter of individual preference. It depends on the size and shape of one's hand and other physical attributes. My personal choice is a baton with an overall length of fifteen to sixteen inches. I also prefer a varnished wooden handle in the shape of a cylinder, about three inches long and five-eighths of an inch in diameter. I have used one like this for thirty years, and it is still as good as new in spite of all the physical abuse it has experienced.

## Holding a Baton

At first, the baton should be held lightly, with the handle in the palm of the hand and supported by the fourth and fifth fingers. The stick should come out of the hand between the second knuckle of the forefinger and the pad of the thumb. The back of the hand should usually be facing upwards. (See the drawing in the diagrams of the beat patterns.) With this posture, the weight of the stick will gently press the handle into the palm of the hand. At times, the fourth and fifth fingers can let go and be relaxed and straightened—for example, in the "get ready" position.

Dexterity in using the baton will grow to the point at which the stick can move up and down as if there were a swivel-pin between thumb and forefinger, allowing the handle to move away from the palm, and snap back into it as the hand rises. We have, in effect, added another flexible joint to the hand. This is another mitigator of physical tension and stress.

Since one may well be conducting a two- or three-hour concert, it is of paramount importance to have a relaxed shoulder, arm, and hand, and to take every opportunity to keep them moving comfortably. If anything locks into a fixed position, it will very soon tire.

## Baton/hand Relationships

With this newly acquired extension of the hand and forearm, we will soon learn that there are three major variations in its behaviour:

1. The hand "leads" the baton, dramatically so when slowing down or signalling a *fermata* or *tenuto*.

2. The hand "moves together with" the baton, for *marcato* or accented sections.

3. The hand "follows" the baton for a more dramatic *marcato*.

Case 1 is the most widely used, Cases 2 and 3 being reserved for less usual situations.

### *Case 1: The Hand Leads*

While holding a baton lightly, try moving the hand up and down six inches, with a cycle time of about one second, while allowing the wrist to flex. You will notice that:

1a. The arm motion is amplified at the hand.

1b. The hand motion is again amplified at the stick.

1c. The motion can be quite smooth for a legato phrase or, if desired, can have a distinct snap—for better definition of the "bounce" and to indicate *staccato*.

## *Case 2: Hand and Baton Move Together*

In Case 2, you will move with a firmer wrist and tighter grip, and you will notice that:

2a.  The hand and arm motion is not amplified. Everything moves together.

2b.  To achieve the same size of movement for visibility purposes, the arm will have to move further than it did in Case 1.

2c.  The motion gives the impression of emphasis or accent.

## *Case 3: The Hand Follows.*

Case 3 is probably the least-used of the three, but it has its occasional uses. Here, the hand follows the baton down in a very vigorous fashion—you move as if you were spearing a fish with the stick.

It can appear, for example, when conducting a final *fortissimo* chord following a held note or rest.

It is also useful for suddenly indicating forceful music after a *pianissimo* section. Imagine two loud "chords of doom" following a quiet, reflective phrase.

Another use of Case 3 could be to signal *sforzando* when adding emphasis in a *marcato* fashion to individual notes.

Case 3 is very dramatic.

# GENERAL BEATING TECHNIQUE

## The Beat—Definition

What is a beat? And how does it relate to the motion of the conductor's baton?

The beat is the pulse which ripples through the music like the ticking of a clock or the dripping of a tap.

It is the moment in time when the drum stick hits the skin or when a note is played. It is the beginning of a sound (or of a silence in the case of a rest).

This moment in time coincides with the conductor's baton, hand, or arm bouncing at the nadir of its journey from one beat to another.

*The bounce or wrist-snap at the bottom of the stick's motion is the precise moment of the striking of the note or the beginning of a rest.*

This is sometimes hard to recognize if one is watching and listening to an orchestra in a concert hall. It can appear as though the music is at odds with the conductor's beat and not synchronising with the bounce. This is because, although the instruments are in fact sounding the notes to coincide with the stick's bounce, the sound waves take time to travel from their source out to the audience. (It is true, however, that some orchestras do occasionally play a fraction of a beat behind the conductor. It's as if no one wants to speak first for fear of not blending in smoothly. Of course, it depends on the type of music, but when this practice is excessive, it can be very tiring for the conductor.)

Another point of confusion arises when one assumes that the motion of the conductor's baton is "down-up." By "down-up" we are really saying that the cycle begins with the arm *descending* such that we have "down to the bounce and up again." This mental image fits well when talking about, and drawing a diagram of, the motion of the hand or baton. (Figures 5 to 11)

However, the motion of the conductor's baton through one complete cycle really begins with the bounce, after which the arm *ascends*. The cycle ends with the next bounce. Therefore, the motion of the conductor's baton is, in fact, an "up-down" motion (i.e., "bounce up, and back down to the next bounce").

(The last two paragraphs may well deserve a second reading, because this concept is central to our discussion of control technique and is difficult to grasp at first.)

For further clarification, let us trace the path of the hand and baton through one cycle.

*From the moment of the beginning of the sound of a beat, when the hand holding the baton will bounce with a wrist-snap at about waist height, the hand will move upward and decelerate until reaching about chin level.*

*From here, it will swing down again and accelerate toward the next wrist-snap, bounce, or beat, at the bottom of its path.*

*The baton has now travelled from one beat to the next during the periodic time of one note or rest.*

This is a very important concept in the discussion of conducting technique, and it will be mentioned later on, when we discuss control.

## Conducting Conventions

When conductors use the generally recognized conducting conventions described in this book—which, incidentally, are quite plain and simple, without unnecessary flourishes and embellishments—it makes it easier for players to read the signals of a variety of conductors. The alternative necessitates having to "get used to" every new conductor encountered.

Sometimes, a player will encounter a series of long multi-rests and is prone to all kinds of distractions while endeavouring to count off time. Under these circumstances, *it is imperative for the player to be able to determine which beat of the measure is being conducted.* Any confusion here could quickly lead to disaster for the player. The conductor's arm movement obviously has to be large enough to be readily visible with peripheral vision and from quite a distance, especially with a large ensemble. The player's ability to accomplish this depends on the conductor's technique as explained below in the section on basic conducting .

## Getting Ready

Getting ready is rather like bringing the troops to attention before giving a marching order. The situation that exists on stage at the commencement of a piece of music affects the conductor's choice of "get ready" commands. If it can be arranged for the conductor to walk onto the stage and find everyone ready to go, it is very effective for him to be able to step onto the podium and immediately conduct a "warning beat" to start the piece. For this to be successful, everyone involved must be completely prepared, warmed up, tuned, comfortably seated or standing, and ready to take the opening breath.

On the other hand, should the stage situation be such that physical preparation is required before the music starts (for example, between chorus numbers in a choral concert, when it may be necessary to change the cast or the set), then a "get ready" signal would be required.

### *Get Ready Signal*

1.  Wait with arms down and relaxed until everybody is in place and ready to go.

2.  Raise both arms in front with hands and baton at a comfortable chest height.

3.  Allow time for choirs to lift and open music or instrumentalists to ready their instruments.

4.  Proceed with the "warning beat(s)."

## The Warning Beat

Warning beats—sometimes called prep beats—can be required at various times during a performance. The periodic time of the warning beat is equivalent to one beat on the metronome marking of the score. It conveys to the ensemble the tempo of the immediately ensuing phrase of music, and therefore a complete beat must be given. For young or beginner members of an ensemble, some conductors count off a whole measure. But, for experienced players, that is not necessary, and the convention is to give only one beat. However, there are instances when one *and a fraction* of a beat are required—for example, when the music starts with a subdivided part of a beat. (See **Complex Warning Beat.**)

To signal with a successful warning beat, the conductor must have a very strong mental image of the next phrase of music, so that the tempo of the warning beat is exactly the tempo of the beats that will follow. Silently singing a short piece of the music to oneself beforehand helps toward an accurate signal. As must continue for the duration of the music, a strong will is required for a successful warning beat. One must avoid being pulled away from the desired tempo by outside influences.

Another requirement of the warning beat is that it convey the required volume. The energy of the beat indicates to the stage or pit whether to sing or play loudly or softly. A vigorous motion calls for a large sound, and a gentle or small motion calls for a small sound. However, "small" must still be big enough to be highly visible.

## Introductory Warning Beat

An introductory warning beat is used to set the music into motion right at the beginning of a piece of music or after a cut that brings everything to a complete stop—as occasionally happens in musical theatre, for dialogue.

## Intermediate Warning Beat

An intermediate warning beat may be necessary during the playing of a piece—for example, after a short pause indicated by the "tracks" sign (cesura). It can also be used to bring in members of the ensemble who have been sitting out with long rests and now have a prominent or solo passage. In this case, the intermediate warning beat is done with the left hand (for a right-handed conductor), while the right hand continues with the regular beating. It provides a great feeling of comfort to the instrumentalist or singer to receive this signal when it is time to rejoin the proceedings and to know that his or her memory and counting are correct. An intermediate warning beat should be easily distinguishable from a regular beat, so that the conductor doesn't appear to be adding a beat to the measure. It need be no more than a small arc of the baton, but it must still, of course, convey the correct periodic time.

For further clarification on this point, see ***Fermata***.

## Variations of the Warning Beat

Warning beats are not all the same. They will vary according to which beat of the measure they are introducing. For example, instead of beginning on the first beat of a measure, some music starts on the last beat. This would require a penultimate beat as the warning beat. Many other situations arise, and these are discussed below in the section on complex warning beats.

*(Conductors of jazz or swing have a rather different convention of warning beat. They often use a verbal addition to the warning beat, such as a spoken full-measure count-off—"One, two, three, four," for example.)*

## A.) "Simple" Warning Beat

I will refer to the last beat of a measure as an "upbeat" and the first beat in a measure as the "downbeat."

For most music, a simple warning beat would be an upbeat leading to play on the first beat (downbeat) of the first measure, as follows:

1. From the "get ready" position, give an inward and upward flick of the right wrist and baton.

2. Continue upward with the baton, hand, and arm to a position in front of the chin.

3. Decelerate the stick, hand, and arm over the top, and let them drop down again for the snap or bounce at the bottom.

It should be noted that the left hand is not necessarily required for this operation. However, it may be added for emphasis on the actual downbeat. (See **LEFT HAND**.)

## B.) "Complex" Warning Beat

A complex warning beat would be used for any of the following situations:

1. The music begins on the upbeat.

2. The music begins on the beat before the upbeat.

3. The music begins on a subdivided part of a beat.

This list covers most situations in current music, but it is just a sampling and does not include every possibility.

*In essence, the conductor will signal the beat immediately prior to the first note to be sounded, except when the note is part of a subdivided note, as in situation 3 above.*

### Example 1

Common time, (4/4) starting on beat 4.

See figure 1.

When the music begins on beat 4 (the upbeat) of a common-time measure, the warning beat will resemble beat 3 (the penultimate beat) of the measure.

A wrist-snap will be followed by an upward motion to the right (beat 3), and the conducting will naturally continue to beat 4, when the ensemble will start to play.

It should be noted that not all members of the ensemble will necessarily start at the beginning. Some will have extra beats to count off before they play. For example, the part for oboe in figure 1 shows a quarter-note rest at beat 4, where the flute starts to play.

Fig. 1

## Example 2a

Common time, (4/4) starting on beat 3.

See figure 2a.

In this example, in which the music begins on beat 3 of a common-time measure, the warning beat will resemble an antepenultimate beat (beat 2 in common time). The wrist-snap will be followed by an upward motion to the left, and the conducting will naturally continue with beats 3 and 4 as the ensemble starts to play.

It should be noted that not all members of the ensemble will necessarily start at the beginning. Some will have some extra beats to count off before they play. For example, the flute music in figure 2a shows rest symbols at the beginning, and the flautists will be watching for the warning beat to know when to start counting. They must be able to reconcile the conductor's signals with their own music to be able to count off correctly until their own entry.

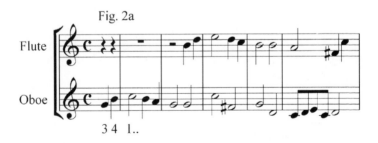

Fig. 2a

**Example 2b**.

(3/4 time.)

See figure 2b.

This example is similar to example 2a except that, in 3/4 time, the antepenultimate beat will be beat 1 in the measure. The wrist-snap will again be followed by an upward motion to the left, and the conducting will naturally continue with beats 2 and 3 as playing begins.

*This demonstrates the important fact that beats 2, 3, and 4 in 4/4 time resemble beats 1, 2, and 3 in 3/4 time.*

The player can therefore always tell how many beats remain until the end of the measure.

In this example, the clarinet must count off two beats after the warning beat.

Fig. 2b

**Example 3**.

(Starting on a subdivided beat in 2/4 time.)

See figure 3.

A complication occurs when the music begins on a subdivided part of a beat. A typical example would be when the music starts with the last eighth-note of a measure in 2/4 time.

As previously stated, to signal the proper tempo, the conductor must give at least one whole beat. In this case, it would be necessary to give one complete beat to convey the desired tempo, *and* an additional fraction of a beat.

We are now thinking in terms of "1 and 2 and," where the music starts on the second "and."

From the "get ready" position, the baton will drop down and bounce up to the right ("1 and"), and will return down to bounce up to the left ("2 and").

The time interval between the bounces establishes the tempo, and the "2" prepares the instrumentalist or singer to start on the final "and."

A left-hand lift at the moment of the final "and" would help to define or emphasize the exact moment of play.

Fig. 3

Clar. in B♭

1and2and    1 and 2 and

# *BASIC CONDUCTING*

*Reprise:*

*From the moment of the beginning of the sound of a beat, when the hand holding the baton bounces with a wrist-snap at about waist height, the hand moves upward and decelerates to about chin level.*

*From here, it will swing down again and accelerate for the next wrist-snap, or beat, at the bottom of its path.*

*The baton has now travelled from one beat to the next during the periodic time of one note or rest.*

*The bounce or wrist-snap at the bottom of the stick's motion, is the precise moment of the striking of the note or the beginning of a rest.*

The simplest form of conducting would be 1, 2, 1, 2, and so on, for a simple march in 2/4 time.

When we conduct with two beats to the bar, we talk of beating "in 2."

"In 2" conducting is used in 2/4, 2/2, cut time, and quick 6/8 time.

The following beating patterns are represented as if the conductor were standing still. In reality, of course, the conductor moves about, turning from side to side to achieve eye contact with various sections of the ensemble or to portray the required mood or emotion. The actual patterns will therefore appear distorted, but, relative to the conductor's shoulders, they are correct.

## Beating in Two

(See figure 5.)

In musical jargon, we refer to the first beat of a measure as the "downbeat" and the last beat of the measure as the "upbeat." These beats really refer to the "bounce" at the bottom of the arm motion, but to describe the beating technique, we have to describe the motion of the arm leading into the bounce.

In describing the arm motion required to define a beat, we are talking in terms of the arm motion being "down-up" (i.e., down to the bounce and back up).

As previously mentioned, however, the arm motion leading up to a beat is really an "up-down" motion (i.e., up from one bounce and down to the next).

We will discuss this later, in the section regarding control.

## Fig. 5 Regular 2/4 Time

Conductor's View

### The Downbeat

For now, I will continue to talk in terms of "down-up."

During beat 1, when beating "in 2," the hand swings down from about chin level while moving slightly to the right of the body, bounces at about waist height (with the bounce defining the moment of the pulse or beat), and up to the right again, back to chin level.

### The Upbeat

The hand then retraces its path in the reverse direction, bounces at the bottom, and finishes where it began in front of the chin, ready for the next downbeat.

This process continues until it is time to stop.

## Beating in Slow 2

Simple "in 2" beating may be modified to improve the handling of a slow rhythm. The variation described below helps to take the stress off the conductor's arm and to make the signals more visible to the ensemble.

The main variation of the "in 2" beating motion for slow time involves raising the hand after the first bounce, continuing on out to the right, around in a large circle, back across the body, and back up the left side, ready for the next downbeat.

It is important to include the little wrist snap at the bottom, because the moment of the pulse would not otherwise be precisely marked by the slow arc of the hand. (See figure 6.)

# Fig.6 Slow 2/4 Time

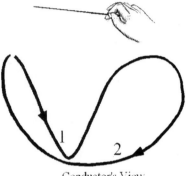

Conductor's View

# PROGRESSING TO 3/4 AND 4/4

## Beating in 3

Before attempting to conduct in 3/4 or 4/4 time—or any other time signature, for that matter—it would be a good idea for you to first learn and practise beating "in 2." It is the easiest format to learn, and it forms the final part of the measure in 3/4 and 4/4 formats.

Having become familiar with beating "in 2," you will be ready to move on to beating "in 3." (See figure 7.)

"In 3" conducting can be used in 3/4, 3/8, and 9/8 time.

From the top of the upbeat, the hand swings down from about chin level, moves to the left side of the conductor's body, bounces at about waist height, and continues in a clockwise circular motion back up to the front of the face.

Now, copying the motion of "in 2" conducting, the hand swings down, moves slightly to the right of the body, bounces at about waist height, and comes up to the right again, to chin level.

From here, the hand retraces its path in the reverse direction (the upbeat) and finishes where it began, in front of the face.

As before, the moment of the beat (the bounce at the bottom or nadir of the curve), should be slightly exaggerated by flicking the baton with the wrist.

That completes one measure, and the hand is ready for the downbeat of the next measure.

Even if the time signature changes, the next measure will still begin with a downbeat, so you will be in the correct position to continue.

## Fig. 7  3/4 Time

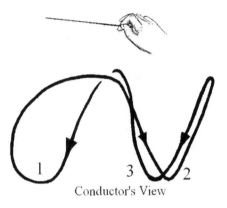

Conductor's View

## Beating in 4

The next pattern to study after "in 3" is "in 4."

(See figure 8.)

## Fig. 8  4/4 Time

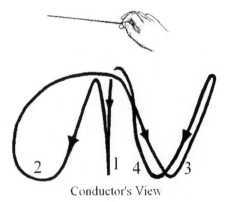

Conductor's View

"In 4" conducting can be used in 4/4 (common time) and 12/8 time. In the case of 12/8 time, each of the four conducted beats counts for a group of three eighth-notes.

"In 4" conducting is instantly recognized by its distinctive downbeat, which it shares with 5/4 time.

From the top of the upbeat, the hand swings down from about chin level *straight down* in front of the body, bounces at about waist height, and comes up again while moving slightly to the *left* of the front of the face.

Now, copying the motion of "in 3" conducting, the hand swings down from about chin level while moving to the left side of the body, bounces at about waist height, and continues in a clockwise circular motion back up to the front of the face.

Copying the motions of both "in 2" and "in 3" conducting, the hand swings down while moving slightly to the right of the body, bounces at about waist height, and comes up to the right again, to chin level.

From here, the hand retraces its path in the reverse direction and finishes where it began, in front of the face.

Remember that the "in 2" downbeat moves to the right and the "in 3" downbeat moves to the left, but **the "in 4" downbeat goes vertically downward.**

In spite of the proliferation of other time signatures in recent compositions, the majority of the available repertoires use mostly 2/2, 6/8, 3/4, or 4/4.

As a piece of music is being played, the downbeat will tell the ensemble, once every measure, whether the conductor is conducting in 2, 3, or 4. **Beware the lazy 4/4 downbeat that bounces to the right instead of the left**. This can precipitate a horizontal figure-eight motion and mislead the ensemble into counting in 2 instead of in 4.

# *OTHER TIME SIGNATURES*

Having mastered the basic "in 2," "in 3," and "in 4" sequences, it is quite easy to adapt them for less-common time signatures.

## 5/4 Time Signature

The next pattern to study after "in 4" is "in 5."

(See figure 9.)

### Fig. 9  5/4 Time

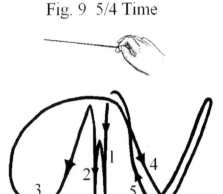

Conductor's View

"In 5" conducting is used with the 5/4 time signature.

It is very similar to 4/4, with the same downbeat, but with the addition of a second, smaller downbeat. From there on, it is like the last three beats of 3/4 or 4/4.

Remember that the "in 2" downbeat moves slightly to the right and the "in 3" downbeat moves slightly to the left, but the "in 4" and "in 5" downbeats go vertically downward.

From the top of the upbeat, the hand swings down from about chin level, straight down in front of the body. It then bounces at about waist height and up again to chest level. After moving two or three inches to the left, the hand swings down again and bounces back up about six inches.

Now, copying the motion of "in 3" conducting, the hand swings down from about chin level while moving to the left side of the body, bounces at about waist height, and continues in a clockwise circular motion back up to the front of the face.

Copying the motions of both "in 2" and "in 3" conducting, the hand then swings down while moving slightly to the right of the body, bounces at about waist height, and comes up to the right again, to chin level.

From here, the hand retraces its path in the reverse direction (the upbeat) and finishes where it began, in front of the face, ready for the next measure.

## 5/8 Time Signature

5/8 time can be conducted using the "in 2" sequence, timing the downbeat for 1, 2, and the upbeat for 3, 4, 5. There will be a proportionate difference in the speed of the downbeats and upbeats.

The rhythm or words of the piece may suggest the reverse order, in which case the downbeat would represent the slower 1, 2, 3, and the upbeat the quicker 4, 5.

In either case, the slower beat can be facilitated by flattening out the arm-motion to be more side-to-side than up-and-down.

## 7/8 Time Signature

7/8 time can be conducted using the "in 3" sequence, timing the downbeat for 1, 2, 3, the second beat for 4, 5, and the upbeat for

6, 7. Once more, there will be a proportionate difference in the speed of the various beats, and again, the rhythm or words of the piece may suggest a different order of the long and shorter beats. In either case, the slower beat can be facilitated by flattening out the arm-motion to be more side-to-side than up-and-down.

## 9/8 Time Signature

9/8 time is quite simple and employs the "in 3" sequence. Each of the three conducted beats accounts for a group of three notes, and each beat will be of equal length.

# THE NEED FOR SUBDIVIDED BEATS

## Largo for 4/4, 3/4, or 6/8 Time Signatures

*Largo* passages of music, which could possibly have a metronome speed as slow as "1/4-note = 40," are difficult to conduct with precision. They are also difficult to play with precision, the tendency being to sound each note too soon.

The solution is the subdivision of the notes, which doubles the effective metronome beat. In the example cited above, the number would increase from 40 to 80, which is far more manageable.

A 4/4 time signature would have eight beats, of which 1, 3, 5, and 7 would be more pronounced than the others. However, the rhythm is usually spoken of as "1, and, 2, and, 3, and, 4, and," where the "and" beats are in fact beats 2, 4, 6, and 8.

A 3/4 time signature would have six beats, of which 1, 3, and 5 would be more pronounced than 2, 4, and 6. In a similar manner, the rhythm is usually spoken of as "1, and, 2, and, 3, and."

A 6/8 time signature, as used in dancing a jig, is normally conducted "in 2," the measure being divided into two groups of three eighth-notes . However, when the tempo within a 6/8 time signature slows sufficiently to make it difficult to conduct "in 2," the beats will be subdivided to make six beats to the bar. The resulting rhythm is different from that of a "slow 3/4" because, with "slow 6/8," the beats are generally more pronounced on 1 and 4.

An example of the conducting pattern for a slow 3/4 passage is shown in figure 10.

## Fig. 10  Slow 3/4

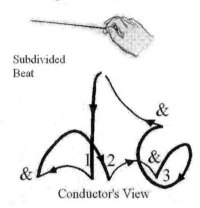

An example of the conducting pattern for a slow 6/8 passage is shown in figure 11.

## Fig. 11  Slow 6/8

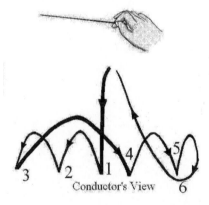

# *CONTROL*

Having learned the basic techniques, the consummate conductor requires one more element to complete his arsenal of skills. That element is control. Control is the ability to bring about infinitely variable changes in the tempo or dynamics of an ensemble in either a gradual or abrupt manner. For the current topic, it is best to think of the arm-motion as being "up-down" rather than "down-up." The first part of the motion is up from the bounce, and this is the part which is most effective in driving change.

The art is in either taking the bounce out or increasing its vigour before the baton ascends once more. The effect for the player is similar to that of a light suddenly going dim or bright— an event of which the eye is acutely aware. Let us explore this further.

## Tempo Changes

### *Fermata*

The most graphic example of this control technique is in the conducting of a passage which includes a *fermata*.

A *fermata* is a musical sign placed above a note to indicate a stop, hold, or pause. It can become a formidable obstacle to the untrained conductor, comparable in its degree of difficulty to negotiating an icy footpath. But, just as ice can become an object of joy to a child who sees the prospect of gleeful foot-sliding, the "formidable *fermata*" can appear to a trained conductor as a welcome opportunity to direct a beautiful, expressive phrase of music.

What's the trick?

First of all, unless it is accompanied by a "tracks" sign, one should **never allow the baton or hand to stop** during the conducting of a *fermata* passage. If the conducting stops, there remains the difficulty of starting again, with resulting uncertainty amongst the players or singers as to whether or not they must wait for a warning beat.

Metaphorically speaking, conducting a *fermata* is like dragging the baton out of a pot of sticky treacle.

It is done this way:

At the moment of the bounce of the beat signalling the note or rest—whichever has the *fermata*—the wrist slowly lifts upwards, dragging the baton slowly behind it. Hence, the bounce disappears and the ensemble is immediately aware of the fact. The slow upward motion might be continued for several seconds. When the stretch in time is sufficient, the speed of the baton, still moving upwards, can now be increased to coincide with the tempo of the ensuing note or phrase, and conducting can continue without a missed beat.

### Fermata Timing Interpretation

Figures 4a and 4b show two different examples of the use of a *fermata*.

Fig. 4a

Violoncello

In figure 4a, the *fermata* is shown above a half-note in a measure with four beats. Does the "sticky treacle" take effect on beat 1 or beat 2? Beat 1 has its own periodic time and deserves to receive its own conducted beat. Therefore, the *fermata* should be conducted on beat 2. The fact that the note is a sustained half-note has no bearing on the conducting. Remember, also, that some members of the ensemble could be *tacet* at this moment and just counting conducted beats. Should the conductor choose to conduct the *fermata* on beat 1, beat 2 would be missing, and there would only be three beats conducted in the 4/4 measure. This would confuse the musicians.

In Figure 4b, the *fermata* is shown on beat 1, but beat 1 is a tied note. The "sticky treacle" must take effect on beat 1. After the desired stretch in time, the conducting can continue on to beats 2, 3, and 4. In this example, the violin will stop at the "and" after 2 and start playing again at the "and" after 3, with two eighth-note rests in the middle.

## Fermata with Tracks

When a *fermata* is followed by the "tracks" sign, the conductor should start as if there were no tracks (again, to get everybody's attention). When the stretch in time is sufficient, a cutoff signal can be made with left, right, or both hands. At this point, the hand or hands should be kept up fairly high, ready to give a small warning beat. Done in this way, the warning beat will not be confused for the next note.

## Tenuto

The treatment of a *tenuto* is similar to that for a *fermata*, but it is for a smaller stretch or hold of a single note. It is used for emphasis or effect before continuing with the regular tempo. This is very useful in *rubato* passages and is used more in singing than in instrumental works.

At the moment of the bounce of the beat that signals the note with the *tenuto* sign above it, the wrist slowly lifts upwards, dragging the baton slowly behind it (the sticky treacle again). Hence, the bounce disappears, and the ensemble is immediately aware of it. As for the *fermata*, when the stretch in time is sufficient, the speed of the baton, still moving upwards, can be increased to coincide with the tempo of the ensuing note or phrase, and conducting can continue smoothly.

## Rallentando or Ritardando

A player has been aware of a sine-wave-like motion of the baton or hand, and has been almost hypnotized into the rhythm, when, all of a sudden, the pattern is broken. The ascending baton appears to stop temporarily at the bounce and then reduce its speed. The player reacts at once to this and has all the rest of the upward motion, plus the downward motion, to make an adjustment in speed before striking the next note. Compare the effectiveness of this with the conductor waiting until the arm is descending before making an adjustment. The latter has little chance of success.

## Accelerando

The same principle applies to the *accelerando* as to the *rallentando* or *ritardando*, except that, for the quicker pace to come, the bounce is magnified and made suddenly quicker. Again, the player reacts at once to this and has the remainder of the upward motion, plus the downward motion, to make an adjustment in speed before striking the next note. Again, compare the effectiveness of this with the conductor waiting until the arm is descending before making an adjustment. The latter has little chance of success.

## Smooth Transition

Composers often incorporate a *rallentando* or *accelerando* just before making a change in tempo. This is encountered quite frequently, especially when an ensemble is playing a selection of numbers from a large work. The following example is from the playing of a medley of Scottish dances.

When changing from a jig with a time signature of 6/8 and metronome speed of "dotted 1/4 note = 120" to a strathspey with a time signature of 4/4 and a metronome speed of "1/4 note = 90," the beat must slow down.

The art of the conductor lies in the ability to use the composer's *rallentando* to smoothly reduce the tempo so that the last beat of the jig has the same tempo as the strathspey. The reverse occurs when changing in the other direction, from strathspey to jig, by using an *accelerando*. Obviously, this device cannot be used when there are dancers dancing the medley. In that case, the change would have to be immediate *(subito)*, without any *rallentando or accelerando*.

# Marcato/Legato

*Marcato* is the term used to describe a passage of music in which the notes are accented and have their own period of decay (i.e., they lose volume from the moment they are struck). In notation, an accent resembling a "greater than" symbol is used. Conversely, *legato* means that the volume of each note remains fairly constant, with very little space between notes.

## Marcato

To indicate that the score is calling for crisp beats—as required to simulate marching feet, for example—the wrist will remain quite stiff. The result is that the bounce is very abrupt and pointed.

The baton, hand, and arm all move up at once. (See Case 2 in the Baton/Hand Relationships section.)

## Legato

The smooth, flowing beats of *legato* music demand a different technique—one in which the stick doesn't lead, but follows a flexing wrist. Instead of the abrupt and pointed bounce signifying *marcato*, the stick motion is relatively smooth, has quite a small bounce and a round bottom, and travels more from side to side.

# The Left Hand

The left hand should rarely be used together with the right hand in a mirror-image sort of conducting. It has its own functions in conducting and should be confined to those.

One good reason for not using the mirrored form of conducting is that the player can literally get his signals crossed. A member of an ensemble needs to see something out of the corner of his eye, moving in a particular direction, to know where the conductor is in the measure. Is it moving from left to right across the conductor's body? Is it moving from right to left across the conductor's body? To see two things moving in opposite directions can be disconcerting, to say the least. However, there are always exceptions.

## 180-Degree Starts
## Wrap-Around Conducting

There are instances when a conductor will be centre-stage, facing an ensemble which wraps right around from the extreme left, to the extreme right. Under these circumstances, with the ensemble forming a semi-circle or more, a two-handed warning beat or upbeat has greater visibility and would be helpful.

Similar circumstances may also present themselves later on in the performance.

With such a large ensemble, the ability for each member to have a frontal view of the conductor is sadly jeopardized, but the wrap-around format should be avoided whenever possible. It certainly helps if the conductor can turn from side to side occasionally, especially when one section or another becomes the dominant section of the moment.

## Various Signals

The left hand has many functions of its own that have to be practised. They are very important in allowing the right hand to continue uninterrupted with its own signals. The reason they need to be practised is that most people find it awkward to do different things with each hand. We can easily discover the difficulty of drawing straight lines across the stomach with one hand while passing the other hand over the head in circles. Young pianists initially have a problem playing with both hands at once, which gets worse when one hand is playing in regular common time while the other must play triplets. Sooner or later, however, it becomes so easy that they forget that it was ever difficult.

## Cueing Entries

When an instrumentalist or singer has been sitting out with a long rest and now has a prominent or solo passage, it is a great feeling of comfort to receive a signal when it is time to rejoin the proceedings. It's also a boost to the musician's confidence to know that his or her memory, and counting, were correct.

This conducting gesture is accomplished with the left hand and consists of:

1.   Pointing toward the soloist or section involved

2.   Giving a distinct warning beat

3.   Giving a left-hand lift for the entry point

The addition of eye contact helps considerably.

## Volume Control

There are several ways to indicate volume changes:

| Required Change | Method | Effectiveness |
|---|---|---|
| *Crescendo* | "Larger" motion of the arm and baton. | Fair |
| *Crescendo* | "Wider" motion of the arm and baton. | Fair |
| *Crescendo* | Left-hand signal. (See below.) | Good |
| *Diminuendo* | "Smaller" motion of the arm and baton. | Fair |
| *Diminuendo* | "Narrower" motion of the arm and baton. | Fair |
| *Diminuendo* | Left-hand signal. (See below.) | Good |
| *Final Diminuendo* | Stop beating and slowly bring the two hands closer together. | Good |

*Note:* Using the left hand for these functions leaves the right arm free to concentrate on other aspects of conducting.

### Crescendo

To increase volume, simply turn the left hand palm-upward and slowly raise it from waist height.

### Diminuendo

To decrease volume, simply turn the left hand palm-downward and slowly lower it from head level to waist height.

## Vibrato

Sections of music requiring dramatic emphasis can be enhanced by increasing the magnitude of *vibrato*. This is another left-hand signal, usually performed by a simulation of the violinist's action of creating *vibrato*.

## Cutoffs

Cutoffs can be signalled with either hand, but there are times when only a part of the ensemble requires a cutoff, while the rest continues to play. Under these circumstances, the cutoff, directed at the appropriate party, is given with the left hand. The right hand continues its normal conducting.

# FINALE

The emphasis of this book has been on *how* conductors do what they do, although *why* they are doing it has occasionally been mentioned. To go further into the analysis of *why* opens up a very special perspective on conducting, and the best way to pursue this analysis is to remove the conductor from the picture and to see what we have left.

The orchestra and/or choir enters the stage and positions itself for the concert. What do they do next? Without a conductor, they must establish some form of cohesion so that they can work together.

Many factors, such as changes in volume, articulation, and rhythm, can be handled easily by experienced musicians, because the directions are clearly marked on the score. All they have to do is listen to everyone else to stay together.

Small chamber groups have learned all the appropriate methods of intercommunication and will have agreed on a leader to give various signals. But, as a group grows in size and complexity, these skills become inadequate.

It is not difficult to list the major obstacles that would be encountered by an orchestra without a conductor. In addition to following the dynamics, the musicians would all have to do the following things together:

1.  Start

2.  Proceed at the correct tempo

3.  Vary the tempo with *rallentandos* or *accelerandos*

4.  Vary the tempo suddenly or gradually

5.  Stretch some notes *(tenuto* or *fermata)*

6.  Hold, stop, and restart *(fermata* with tracks)

7.  Finish

Note that these seven items deal with starting, stopping, and tempo. Of these seven items, we should zero in on numbers 5 and 6 as being the most difficult to control, and therefore demanding the most attention. For emphasis, I would like to reprise here my earlier suggestions for control, which appeared under the headings of *fermata* and *tenuto*.

> A.) *"For the current discussion, it is best to think of the arm-motion as 'up-down.' The first part of the motion is up from the bounce, and this is the part which is most effective in driving change. **The art is to take out the bounce, or increase its vigour, before the baton once more ascends**. The effect for the player is similar to that of a light suddenly going dim or bright—an event of which the eye is acutely aware."*

> B) *"First of all, one should **never allow the baton or hand to stop** during the conducting of a passage with a* fermata. *If the conducting stops, there remains the difficulty of starting again, with resulting uncertainty amongst the players or singers as to whether they must wait for a warning beat."*

> C.) *"Metaphorically speaking, conducting a* fermata *is **like dragging the baton out of a pot of sticky treacle**."*

# FINAL CADENCE

Conducting is a very rewarding experience, especially when a performance is very successful and enjoyed by the audience. The conductor and musicians become highly dependent on each other. They become a team, and the conductor fills the role of facilitator. As a leader, it is one thing to not be understood, and a very different thing to be misunderstood. One must avoid, at all costs, sending confusing signals, whether or not one's intentions are good. A typical example of this would be when a conductor tries to conduct the rhythm rather than the basic beat. Imagine one section of the ensemble working on straight quarter-notes while another section plays an occasional *haemeola* (hemeola), triplet, or offbeat rhythm. If the conductor suddenly switched to conducting one of the other rhythms in an attempt to help that group, the rest of the ensemble would not know where the regular beat was. It is at these moments that the conductor has to keep it simple. He must stay with the beat, delegate responsibility, and trust the players or singers to read their parts correctly. Of course, any potential problems of this sort would ideally be resolved during rehearsals.

One final thought. Practice leads to confidence, and confidence leads to a more relaxed, enjoyable, and polished performance. If you enjoy your conducting, your emotion will be relayed to your ensemble, everything will turn out well, and the audience will love it!

# APPENDIX

## *ITALIAN TEXT*

This partial Italian-to-English dictionary includes the majority of the Italian words in published music scores. When used by a composer, they are suggested directions for mood, emotion, or style.

In the case of tempo, composers can be more exact by using metronome markings, but have traditionally used words such as *Allegro*—which literally means cheerful, happy, or gay. Depending on the character of the music, the tempo suggested by these moods could vary considerably, and sometimes a word may have a modifier (e.g., *Allegro moderato* or *Allegro fuoco*). However, the basic words are generally accepted as being in the order as shown in the table below, from *very slow* to *very fast*.

### The definite article "the"

|            | Singular   | Plural  |
|------------|------------|---------|
| Masculine: | il  lo  l' | i  gli  |
| Feminine:  | la  l'     | le      |

### The indefinite article "a" or "an"

| Masculine: | un  uno   |
|------------|-----------|
| Feminine:  | una  un'  |

| Tempo | | Translation |
|---|---|---|
| *very* | Larghissimo | Very broad, very slow |
| *slow* | Largo | Broad, slow |
| | Larghetto | A little less than broad |
| | Grave | Serious, grave |
| | Lento | Slow |
| | Adagio | Easily, slowly |
| | Adagietto | A little easy |
| | Andante | Walking pace |
| | Andantino | A faster walking pace |
| | Moderato | Moderately |
| | Allegretto | A little cheerful, gay |
| | Allegro | Cheerful, gay |
| | Vivace | Vivacious, lively |
| | Veloce | Fast, quick |
| *very* | Presto | Quickly, soon |
| *fast* | Prestissimo | Very quickly, very soon |

# DICTIONARY

## A

a—to, in, as, at, until

a cappella—as in the chapel, unaccompanied

a capriccio—as whimsical, flighty

a tempo—return to tempo

accelerando—increase tempo

acciaccatura—crushed, (now, generally used for short appoggiatura, with line through)

adagio—Slowly, easily

ad libitum (ad lib.)—at will

affabile—pleasant, civil

affettuoso—affectionate, feeling, tender

affrettando—urging, hastening, with emotional pressure

agitato—upset, excited

al fine—to the finish or end, marked "fine"

al, alla, alle—to the

allargando—extended, slower

allegretto—a little slower than allegro

allegro—cheerful, gay, fairly quick

allegro assai—much cheerfulness, faster then allegro

allegro giusto—quick and with precision

allegro moderato—moderated or tempered allegro

altissimo—very high

amabile—friendly, lovable

amore—love, affection, tenderness

amoroso—amorous, affectionate, fond

andante—a strolling, walking pace

andantino—little andante (now, slightly faster than andante)

andare—to go on

Anglaise—in an English style

anima—soul

animato—animated, lively

animoso—bold, evil

antico—ancient

appassionato—impassioned, with fervour

appenato—penned or written

appoggiato—assisted, supported

appoggiatura—leaning, long grace note of varying length

arco—play with the bow (return from pizzicato)

ardente—with fire, burning passion

ardore—ardently

arioso—light, airy

arpeggio—notes of a chord played consecutively

assai—enough, very

assai piu—much more

attacca—proceed to next section with negligible pause

# B

ballabile—suitable for dancing

barocco—baroque, bizarre

bassa—low, deep

basso—bass, the lowest voice

basso continuo—an instrument or score dedicated to the bass accompaniment

battaglia—a battle

bel canto—beautiful singing, eighteenth-century in Italy

bene, ben—good, well

ben marcato—well accented

bis—twice

bravo—skillful, congratulatory applause

bravura—skill, courage

breve—a double whole-note, two semi-breves

brillante—bright, sparkling

brio—vivacity, spirit

brusquamente—roughly, abruptly

buffa, buffo—comic, funny

burlando—poking fun, playful

# C

cadenza—ornamental passage to conclude a solo

calando—scaling down

calmato—tranquil

caloroso—warm

cambiare—change, as to the next instrument

cantabile—in a fashion suggesting singing

cantando—singing along

canto—song, singing

capo—head, top

cappella—chapel

carezzando—caressing, coaxing

carita—charity, mercy

celere—quick

cesura, caesura—stop (to the conductor, cutoff)

cembalo—harpsichord, tambourine

coda—a supplement to conclude a piece

col—with the

coll'arco—with the bow

colla voce—with the voice, take lead from the voice

coloratura—agile, colourful, ornamental vocal line

come prima—as before

come—as, like

comodo—comfortable, unrestrained, convenient

con sordino, sordini—with mute(s)

con—with

concento—harmony

concertino—small concerto, or the solo instrument

concerto—a work for solo instrument(s) and orchestra

concerto grosso—baroque concerto with group of solos

continuo—see basso continuo

contralto—the deepest female voice

coperti—covered, a drum muted with cloth

corde—string

crescendo—increasing volume

# D

da capo (D.C.)—from the top or beginning

da capo al fine—from the top and to the word "fine"

da, dal, dalle, dalla—from, by, at, as

dal segno (D.S.)—from the sign

debole—weak, feeble

deciso—decided, with resolve

decrescendo—becoming softer

delicato—delicate

destra—right, as in right hand

devoto—devout, pious

di molto—very much

di—of, about, from, any, by, at

difficile—difficult

dignitoso—dignified

diluendo—weakening, diluting

diminuendo (dim.)—softening

discreto—fair, discreet

di sopra—from above

disperato—desperation

divisi—divide the chord

dolce—sweet, soft

dolente—aching, sorry

dolore—to cause sorrow

doloroso—sorrowful

dopo—after, later

doppio movimento—twice the speed

doppio—double

drammatico—dramatic

due corde—on two strings

duo—duet, duo, in two parts

duolo—suffering, grief

duro—hard, tough

# E

e, ed—and

elegante, eleganza—smart, elegant

elegiaco—lamenting, elegiac

emozione—emotion, excitement

energico—vigorous, resolute

enfatico—emphatic, bombastic

epico—heroic

equabilemente—equably, steadily, constantly

equamente—fairly, justly

espirando—last breath, expiring

espressivo—clear, meaningful, with expression

estinto—extinct, dead

# F

facile—easy

fantastico—fanciful, marvellous, eccentric

fastoso—pompous

fermamente—steadfastly, resolutely

fermata—a sign to indicate stop, hold, or stretch

feroce—ferocious, wild

fervente—fervent, with great warmth of feeling

fervido—fervent, ardent

festivo—festive, gay

festoso—festive, merry

fiacco—weak, lazy

fieramente—fiercely

fine—finish, end

flebile—mournful, wailing

forte possible—as loud as possible—*fff*

forte—strong, loud—*f*

forte-piano—loud, then immediately soft—*fp*

fortissimo—extra loud—*ff*

forza—force, power

forzando—sudden emphasis or accent—*fz*

freddezza—coolness, coldness

frescamente—freshly, coolly

fretta—hurry, haste

fugal—in fugal style

fugue—in contrapuntal style with more than one voice

funebre—funereal

fuoco—fire, passion

furioso—furiously, madly

furore—wrath, rage

## G

gaio—merry, gay

galante—polite, courteous

garbo, garbato—polite

generoso—generous, dignified

gentile—polite, kind

giocando—playful

giocoso, giojoso—facetious, jocular

giubilante—jubilant, exultant

giustezza—exactness, correctness

giusto—correct, precise, strict

glissando—rapid scale slurring over keys

gradevole—pleasant, nice

gradualmente—gradually

grandioso—grand, noble

grave—very slow and solemn

grazioso—graceful, grand style

grosso—full, large

grottesco—grotesque

guitto—strolling player, ham actor

gusto—taste, flavour

# I

il, i—the (see "The definite article" above this list.)

imitando—imitating

imitato—imitated

impaziamente—impatiently

imperioso—arrogant

impetuoso—impetuous

imponente—imposing

in—in, into, at, by, to

inquieto—restless, upset

intimo—intimate, private

intrepidamente—fearlessly, boldly

irato—angry, wrathful

ironico—ironic, sarcastic

irresoluto—wavering, unresolved

# J

joioso—joyous

jubiloso—exulting

# L

lacrimoso—tearful, weeping

lamentando—regretful

lamentoso—sorrowful

languendo—failing, languishing

languido—languid, listless

largemente—broadly

larghetto—a little faster than largo

largo—easy going, broad

le, la—the (see "The definite article")

legatissimo—very smooth

legato—smooth

leggiero, leggero—lightly

legno—the wood of the bow

lentando—slowing down

lento—slow

lestamente—quickly, nimbly

lesto—lively, quick

l'istesso—the same

libretto—book of words to a musical play

loco—place, return to original octave

lontano—distant, absent

lugubre—exaggerated, with gloominess

lunga pausa—long pause

lusingando—cajoling, flattering

luttuoso—sad, sorrowful, mournful

## M

ma—but

ma non troppo—but not too much

maestoso—majestic, regal

maggiore—greater, major

mano—hand

mano destra—right hand

mano sinistra—left hand

marcato—marked, prominent

martellato—hammered

marziale—martial

meno—less

mesto, mestoso—unhappy, melancholy

mezzo forte—half-strong, moderately loud—*mf*

mezzo, mezza—half

mezzo piano—half-gentle, moderately soft—*mp*

mezzo soprano—voice between soprano and contralto

minacciando—threatening

minaccioso—menacing

misterioso—mysterious

misurato—strict, measured time

mobile—flighty, undependable

moderato—moderate

molto—much

morendo—dying away

mormoroso—murmuring

mosso—moving, speed

moto—motion

moto perpetuo—perpetual motion

movimento—movement, hustle

## N

negligente—heedless, negligent, lax

nel, nella, nell'—in the, at the

nobile—noble, grand

non—no, not

## O

obbligato—indispensable, required, counterpoint melody

opus—work, composition

ossia—or else, alternative

ostinato—obstinate, continuous, unceasing

ottava—octave, eighth

ottava alta—octave higher

ottava bassa—octave lower

## P

parlando, parlante—sung in a speaking manner

passionato—passionate

passionatamente—passionately

patetica—pathetic

pateticamente—pathetically

pausa—a pause

paventoso—fearful

per—for, from, through, in order to, etc.

perdendosi—gradually decreasing in time and tone

pesante—heavy

piacere—pleasure

piacevole—agreeable, suave, delicate

piangevole—mournful

pianissimo—very soft—*pp*

piano—soft—*p*

piena, pieno—full

pieta—pity, mercy

pietoso—pitiful, merciful

piu—more

piu mosso, piu moto—more motion

pizzicato—plucked with the fingers

placido—calm, placid

poco a poco—little by little

poi—then

pomposo—pompous

ponderoso—weighty, ponderous

ponticello—bridge supporting the strings

possibile—possible

precipitato—rash, hasty

precipitando—hurriedly

precisione—precision

preciso—precise, exact

prestissimo—very quickly, very early

presto—quickly, rapidly, early, soon

primo, prima—first, prime, before

prima donna—first lady, leading female role

# Q

quasi—almost, copying the manner

quieto—quiet, peaceful, shy, retiring

# R

rallentando—slow down gradually

rapidamente—rapidly, quickly

rattenuto—hold back, stretch

religioso—devout, solemn

replicazione—repeat

rigore—strictness

rinforzando—reinforced

ripetizione—repeated

risoluto—resolved, firm

ritardando—slow down quite quickly

ritenuto—slow down suddenly, hold back

rubato—robbed, vary tempo from solid accompaniment

rustico—rustic, rural

## S

scherzando—playful, mischievous

schietto—frank, sincere

scordatura—mistuning of strings

se—if

secco—dry, sharp, cold

segno—sign

segue—continue to following

semplice—simple, plain

sempre—ever, always

sentimento—feeling

senza—without

serioso—serious

sforzando—sudden emphasis, strained, sharply accented

simile—alike, similar

sinistra—left

smorzando—deaden or tone down the sound

soave—soft, sweet

solenne—serious, solemn

solo—alone, one person only

sonore—resonant

sordino—a mute or damper

sostenuto—maintained, sustained

sotto—subdued

sotto voce—soft voice, under the voice

spianato—smooth, even

spiccato—picked, plucked

spirito—with spirit or life

stabile—stable, constant

staccato—detached, separated, shortened length

stanchezza—fatigue, exhaustion

stentato—forced

stesso—same, very same

strascinato—dragging behind

strepitoso—noisy, resounding

stringendo—pressing forward, acceleration

su, sul, sull, sulla etc.—on, over, above

suavita—sweet, delicate

subito—sudden, rapid

sussurando—sigh, whisper

svelto—alert, quick

# T

tacet—quiet, silent

tanto—so much

tardamente—lagging, slowly

tema—subject, theme

tempo—time, speed

tempo giusto—correct or exact time

tempo ordinario—ordinary or common time

tempo primo—the original or beginning tempo

tempo rubato—robbed time, irregular time

teneramente—caringly

tenuto—held, stretched, lengthened

tessitura—average range of a part, particularly vocal

timoros—timid, fearful

tosto—immediately, soon

tranquillo—calm, peaceful

trascinando—dragging the time

tre—three

tre corde—three strings, no soft-pedal

tremolo—quivering, rapid repetition of one note, (*voice*, long wobbly, oscillations of pitch)

trio—three performers

trionfale—triumphant

tristezza—sadness, sorrow

troppo—too, too much

tutti—all

# U

uguale—equal

una corde—a chord, one string, soft-pedal on piano

# V

va—to go

vago—vague

veloce—fast, speedy

velocissimo—extreme rapidity

vibrato—a slight undulation in pitch and modulation

vigoroso—vigorous, energetic

violente—violent, bestial

vitamente—lively

vivace—vivacious, lively

vivo—alive, animated

volta prima—first time

volta seconda—second time

volta—time

volti subito (V.S.)—turn page quickly

volti—turn (the page)

# REFERENCE BOOKS

The following books are listed for the benefit of those music-lovers who have the time and desire to do further research in any of the numerous aspects of music and related subjects.

I have included an "Italian to English" dictionary because of Italian's tremendous influence on the language of text associated with music. The Internet is not to be ignored as a vast resource of historical data regarding compositions, composers, lyricists, instrumentalists, and singers.

Anderson, W. R., Harrison, Julius., Dent J. Edward., Toye, Francis., Hussey, Dyneley., Evans, Edwin., Bonavia, F., and Blom, Eric. *The Music Companion.* London, England: Victor Gallancz. 1954.

Gray, Anne. *The Popular Guide to Classical Music.* New York: Carol Publishing Group. 1993.

Bagar, Robert and Biancolli, Louis. *The Concert Companion.* New York: McGraw-Hill. 1947.

Anderson, Keith. *The ABC of Classical Music.* Naxos. Undated.

Hopkins, Anthony. *The Dent Concertgoer's Companion.* London, England. Orion Publishing Group. 1993.

Morin, Alexander. *Classical Music.* San Francisco, CA. Backbeat books. 2002.

Latham, Alison. *The Oxford Companion to Music*. Oxford, England. Oxford university press. 2002.

Blom, Eric, and Cummings, David. *The New Everyman Dictionary of Music*. Markham, Ontario. J. M. Dent & sons. 1988.

Ragazzini, Giuseppe. *Harper's Shorter Italian Dictionary*. Bologna, Italy. Zanichelli. 1989.

# ABOUT THE AUTHOR

John Watkins is a pianist, oboist, singer, freelance conductor, music arranger, and founding member of The Scarborough Bel Canto Choir. A retired professional engineer, he uses his keen analytical skills to bring a sharp focus to a seemingly complex and mysterious subject.

978-0-595-43396-4
0-595-43396-0

Printed in Great Britain
by Amazon.co.uk, Ltd.,
Marston Gate.